IMAGES
of England

FARNHAM

THE SECOND SELECTION

This map of the Farnham area is around 150 years old. Hale is written as Heal, Weybourne as Weyburn, Coxbridge is depicted as Cocks Bridge and Wrecclesham is shown as Wraccklesham. Rowledge was too small, and insignificant, to even merit a mention.

IMAGES
of England

FARNHAM
THE SECOND SELECTION

Jean Parratt

TEMPUS

Here in the ancient coaching inn yard of the Lion and Lamb Hotel, showing both the listed barn occupied by Laura Ashley and a modern unit in the background topped by the *Mary Rose*, flagship of King Henry VIII, Monseigneur Bruce Kent (*left foreground*), on a sponsored CND walk from Aldermaston to Burghfield, stops to chat to internationally acclaimed potter Siddiq El'nigoumi (*right foreground*).

This book is dedicated to the town's journalists and photographers of the past and to the 'characters' it once had – amongst them Annie Martin, Bill Eames, Harold Cole, Charlie and Matt Wenham, 'Miss' Margaret and Old Bill. Their legacy is a woven tapestry of the written word, the informative picture and the colour of legend, truth, apocryphal stories and, on occasions, a thread of eccentricity – the whole making Farnham's social history.

First published 2003

Tempus Publishing Limited
The Mill, Brimscombe Port,
Stroud, Gloucestershire, GL5 2QG

British Library Cataloguing in Publication Data.
A catalogue record for this book is available from the British Library.

ISBN 0 7524 2682 6

Typesetting and origination by Tempus Publishing Limited
Printed in Great Britain by Midway Colour Print, Wiltshire

Contents

About the Author

Jean Parratt, although a Londoner by birth, has taken Farnham to her heart. After moving to the town in the late 1940s, she attended Farnham Girls' Grammar School for the last years of her secondary education. After employment in a bookshop and a short spell in local journalism before marriage to a Farnham man, she later became involved in education when her three children were young. In 1980 she returned to journalism in London, later working on two newspapers in Farnham. At the same time she continued with her interest in history, lecturing to both adults and children with her private collection known as the 'Museum on a Shoestring'.

Jean has appeared many times on television and radio and still writes in a freelance capacity for newspapers and magazines. This is her ninth published book.

Although now a senior citizen, she remains a presenter for *Talking Newspaper for the Blind*, is an ardent supporter of ARC – the organization for research into rheumatism and arthritis, runs a museum club for 100 children a month, is a member of the education team at the Museum of Farnham and is a wife, mother and grandmother.

Acknowledgements

I should like to thank the following people for their help and kindness, especially those who loaned pictures for publication in this volume: Audrey and Bill Wenham, Mike Leishman, Pete Wisbey, Rosemary Jones, Randal Bingley, Mrs Mary Vincent, Esmé and Tom Martin, Guy Bellamy, Bill Wallis, John Wallinder, Mike and Carol Weeks, Moira Partridge, the Wilson family, Jim Bodkin, Chris Hellier, Robin Broatch, Mary and Roy Collins, Cecil 'Dick' Ridgers, the late Bill Eames, Derek and Norman Elkins, Marion and Don Banks, Malcolm Miller, Mary Myers, Rosalind Crowe, Cyril Trust, Kathy Hammond, Barbara Wills, Irene Watt, the late Edward Griffith, Wendy Hobart, Tim Humphrey, Maria Farrow, Julian Rolliston, Helen Cranstone, Dalwyn Smart, the late Bill Ewbank Smith, Gladys Farmer, Nellie Hawkins, Dorothy French, Simmons Aerofilms Limited, Anne Jones at the Museum of Farnham and my husband, Ted, for the scanning and keeping my computer going. Should I have failed to acknowledge anyone I apologize and will rectify the matter at a later date.

Introduction

There can be few country locations which have had more books written about them than Farnham in Surrey, a market town on the Surrey/Hampshire border where men, women and children have dwelt for at least 8,000 years. A visitor to the area can appreciate, almost immediately, the sense of history which pervades it, and a visit to the town's museum will confirm immediately that Farnham is no ordinary place, but one where the present meets the past, literally face-to-face.

Samuel Johnson said: 'When a man is tired of London, he is tired of life; for there is in London all that life can afford.' I would suggest that this could be paraphrased to read: 'When a person is tired of finding out about Farnham, he or she is tired of life; for there is in Farnham's history more than can ever be assimilated.' I hope to introduce a person new to the area to a potted history of the town's major points of interest, and to those who know it well, I trust that much that is new to them will be revealed in the following pages, both through the images and the accompanying captions.

Farnham, a Town of Firsts

Farnham is a town with many records, both of 'firsts' and superlatives. Around 8,000 years ago our Middle Stone Age ancestors dug pits close to the present Six Bells roundabout and lived in them because they had a good supply of water from the river nearby, vast quantities of wood and unlimited supplies of material from which to make their flint tools. These 'pit dwellings' were found in the 1930s by the headmaster of Badshot Lea school, which is less than a mile from the site. Known locally as 'Professor', Mr W.F. Rankine, who took a keen interest in archaeology, rewarded his pupils if they found flint tools and took them to him. When he suddenly found himself handing out more coins than usual he asked the youngster from whence their present finds had come? They led him to the place, just a couple of hundred yards from the Six Bells public house. The site was then excavated and W.F. Rankine recorded his finds in the *Surrey Archaeological Collections*, volume XXXIV, 1936.

In 1937-38 the site was excavated scientifically, and for the first time in this country a complete Mesolithic flint industry was located. The finds were divided amongst the British Museum, Guildford Museum and the University Museum of Archaeology and Ethnology at Cambridge. Farnham did not have a permanent museum at that time. The pit dwellings are the largest group found to date, and thus the site now occupied by grazing horses and adjacent to the sewage treatment works has been designated as the oldest village in this country.

Until the mid-1960s, the river which had attracted the Mesolithic people frequently broke its banks and flooded the nearby fields, making them fertile and often very damp – ideal conditions for ferns to flourish. It is from these ferns that the town derived its name in Saxon times – Fearnehamme, a hamlet surrounded by ferns.

From the Middle Stone Age onwards there is evidence that the place we now call Farnham has been continually inhabited. The Romans built a substantial bath and villa just yards from the Mesolithic pit dwellings and, interestingly, members of another European nationality, Germans, who were prisoners-of-war and billeted at Runfold, were given the task of excavating the remains of these buildings in the winter of 1946/47. Evidence of a Roman pottery kiln was found at the site of the sewage treatment works, another kiln was discovered at Snailslynch (about 800 yards from the Roman bath) and several others were located on the south side of the town.

In 1138 Henri de Blois, Bishop of Winchester, started building a castle at Farnham, a town roughly halfway between London and Winchester. Ten years earlier the first Cistercian monastery in this country had been founded at Waverley, on a bend of the river, just over a mile from the present town centre, and by the fourteenth century it was probably the most important monastery in England.

These two major buildings, on such an important trade route, resulted in Farnham being a well-used stopover point for travellers, in particular members of the Royal Family. Mary Tudor stayed at Farnham Castle on her way to marry Philip of Spain at Winchester Cathedral; Queen Elizabeth I slept at the castle on several occasions and so frequently did King Charles II stay there when Bishop Morley held the bishopric that the cleric is alleged to have written: 'The King and his brother abused my hospitality at Farnham... and used the Castle as an Inn.' One King, Charles I, spent his last night of freedom in Farnham before going on to London and his execution. A green ceramic plaque on the wall of Vernon House, West Street, gives details of this brief visit – when a King stayed in an ordinary town house instead of a palace or a castle.

Farnham Castle has seldom witnessed conflict, although for ten months in 1216, Louis, Dauphin of France, after having landed in England, rapidly took Guildford, Farnham and Winchester until the castle was re-taken by William Marshall, Earl of Pembroke. During the Civil War the castle was, except for two short periods, in the hands of the Parliamentary forces.

The Local Studies Library at the Museum of Farnham contains many books and leaflets giving information about Waverley Abbey and Farnham Castle, anyone wanting to learn more about these important buildings (the former now only a ruin but the latter in regular use as the Centre for International Briefing) can find all the information he or she may require at this museum.

In addition to money generated by wealthy visitors, the residents of Farnham have been fortunate in the quality of the land around the town, at first promoting the grazing of sheep and thus a big woollen industry, later used for the growing of wheat and as a meeting place for farmers from Hampshire and Sussex who stopped in Farnham on their way to markets in London, and finally as a place where hops thrived. At one time, Farnham hops were said to be the most expensive in this country – some reports even state, 'the most expensive in the world.' Hops lead to brewing, brewing leads to public houses and, at one time, Farnham is said to have had more hostelries per head of population than any other town in the country.

The coming of the railway in 1848 changed the lives of Farnham people forever. Instead of relying on local industries it was now possible for those men with the necessary skills to work in London and still live in Farnham. It took scarcely any longer to reach the metropolis 150 years ago than it does today and some might say, sarcastically, that the journey takes much longer now, especially when leaves are on the line or there is the wrong kind of snow. Both of these excuses have been given regularly over the railway public address system on the Waterloo to Alton route, which includes a stop at Farnham.

In 1859 Farnham had a newspaper, the broadsheet *Surrey and Hants News*, which was written, published and printed in the town. It was owned by Mr Arthur Lucy, who operated from 1, The Borough. In 1892 Mr Ernest Langham started the *Farnham Herald*, a very small paper hardly larger than A4 format, and, by way of attracting customers, he gave his newspaper away for the first six months of its publication. Then he charged a halfpenny a copy. It is interesting to note that, in 2002, both newspaper titles are now owned by the same man, Sir Ray Tindle, but both the financial aspect and sizes are reversed – the *Surrey and Hants News* is tabloid and free whilst the *Farnham Herald* is broadsheet and costs almost 200 times as much as the purchase price just over a century ago – an increase roughly parallel with the improvement of wages during the same period.

Education and religion have played major roles in the life of Farnham residents – there has been a grammar school for boys in the town for four centuries – and in addition to St Andrew's parish church, where people have prayed for over 1,200 years, the town has had its Dissenters for at least 300 years, many groups of which met in private houses and corrugated iron huts to worship. Farnham's first Roman Catholic church, dedicated to St Polycarp, was situated in Bear Lane (next to the town's first police station) in the late nineteenth century. Today there are at least forty churches, chapels and meeting places in the town and its immediate environs.

The area is well served for schools, both state and private, with some, such as Frensham Heights, known nationally. Its students have included, over the years, the sons and daughters of actors, authors, broadcasters and musicians of international repute.

The aroma exuded by the pine trees, which grow in abundance around the town, might seem conducive to firing the imagination or sharpening the word-power of potential writers, because Farnham has had more than its fair share of literary men and women. From Izaak Walton (who wrote *The Compleat Angler* whilst living at Farnham Castle) and Jonathan Swift (satirist and author of *Gulliver's Travels* who penned other works when acting as a secretary to Sir William Temple at Moor Park House) through to J.M. Barrie, whose masterpiece *Peter Pan* was born in this town. Then, in more recent times, have been W. Somerset Maugham, Brian Vesey Fitzgerald, Ken Follett, Frederick Forsyth, Guy Bellamy and Joanna Trollope (who was also a teacher at Farnham Girls' Grammar School). All these, and many more, wrote internationally published volumes whilst living in this town.

It is not only in the literary world that Farnham has excelled. Personalities in other fields have been born, bred or lived in the town or its environs, including: Tommy Reilly (harmonica player); Cyril Garbett (Archbishop of York); Ron Ridout (*Guinness Book of Records* holder for greatest number of textbooks published); Jeffrey Tate (international music conductor); Liza Goddard (actress and former pupil at Farnham Girls' Grammar school); Trevor Macdonald, David Rose, Alastair Stewart and Desmond Hamill (television newsreaders); Lord Montgomery (British Army Field Marshal in the Second World War); Olive Edis (the only female photographer allowed into France in the aftermath of the First World War); John Noakes (of television's *Blue Peter* programme); Jessie Matthews (music hall star, Mrs Dale of *Mrs Dale's Diary* on the radio and one-time licensee of a former Farnham public house); Vera Lynn (the Forces' Sweetheart of World War Two and beyond); Peter Pears (singer); Admiral Sir William James (the subject of Sir John Millais' famous painting 'Bubbles'); Kate O'Mara (film star); Jeremy Hardy (broadcaster and activist); Bill Wallis (Shakespearian and comedy actor) and Graham Thorpe (England Test Match cricketer). Cyril Garbett, Ron Ridout, Jeffrey Tate, Guy Bellamy, Bill Wallis and Jeremy Hardy are all former Farnham Grammar School pupils.

A two-seater, petrol-driven car, built in Farnham, is on display at the Beaulieu Motor Museum, as one of the first such vehicles on the roads of Britain – it was constructed at 50 West Street by John Henry Knight, who was also believed to be the first person in this country, in 1895, to receive a fine for a motoring offence. Still with motoring, it was John Michael (Mike) Hawthorn who was the first person to bring the World Motor Racing Driving Championship to this country in 1958. He was killed a few months later when his vehicle left the road and crashed into a tree, just outside Guildford.

Farnham is said to have more ghosts than any other town in this country and it is also the birthplace of William Willett, the man who instigated Daylight Saving. It is the town in which it is believed the first ever Two-Minute Silence took place, in May 1916 and, from 1919, internationally observed on 11 November, the day in 1918 when the Armistice was signed. It was in Farnham, too, that the hammer-beam roof of Westminster Hall was constructed, by Hugh Herland, in 1396-97, although it was not completely installed in London – where it remains – until 1400.

Today Farnham is still a thriving town, one where there are many courtyards leading from the main streets and just waiting to be explored. It is a town which offers much to do in the day but little in the evening, apart from drinking in one of the many public houses and hotels, rehearsing at one of several dramatic and opera societies, having membership of one of the vast range of clubs and organizations, eating in one of its twenty or more restaurants or being educated at an exceptionally broad-based adult education unit. However, with such beautiful countryside in which to walk on the town's outskirts and, on the whole, large gardens to be tended, is there really time for anything else except to settle down with a good book just before going to bed?

I do not originate from Farnham, although part of my education took place here, and I have only been a resident for just over a half-century. However, my husband's family have lived here since the mid-eighteenth century and so the name I took upon marriage is so much part of the area that I, too, feel I am an integral part of the town I have adopted.

When I am tired of Farnham I will be tired of life and I would encourage everyone to really investigate the riches with which this town is endowed: its history, its architecture and, in particular, its pensioners. Most of them have a wealth of interesting, if sometimes apocryphal, stories about a Fourteen-penny House, a white witch known as Mother Ludlam, an eccentric cave-dweller known as Father Foot, a ghost named Rotca who skated after dark in an empty rink and an elephant who stole a loaf of bread through a baker's upper window when it was en route to a circus venue. Listen to them, jot down their tales, then investigate for yourself. Then you, like me, may be able to locate the fourteenth-century building in West Street where men, lying on their stomachs on a false ceiling over a stable, were able to signal to the soldiers in the keep at Farnham Castle during the Civil War. This is a 'word-of-mouth' story, which has been handed down for more than 300 years, yet, to the best of my investigation, knowledge and belief, it is true.

One
Family Ties

The Vanner family about 1905, left to right: Rosamund Helen, Patrick Archibald on the lap of his father, James Saunders, Richard Thomas, Mary Ann (*née* Martin), Reginald James and Daisy Mary. All the children went to Wrecclesham school and the boys later attended Farnham Grammar School, where Reg and Patrick played in the school's 1st XI at both football and cricket. All three boys played for 'The Bungs' (Farnham United Breweries football team), and Richard also played for Aldershot and later Tottenham Hotspur. The girls married George and Percy Parratt from an adjacent farm. Percy and Daisy later moved to New Zealand, where her brother, Reginald, also emigrated.

Opposite: James Elkins was born at Wrecclesham in 1823. His first wife, Sophia Caesar, whom he married on 2 October 1847, died nineteen months later on 26 May 1849. His second wife was Lucy Trussler, born in 1831, whom he married five years and one week after his first nuptials. The couple then had a very long partnership before he died in July 1915. Lucy, who had obviously been a very hardworking wife, judging by the number of patches and darns on James' jacket, lived on at their home, Recreation Cottage, Rowledge, until 1922.

Right: When Bertram Elkins, who had been born at Oakfield Cottages, adjacent to Wrecclesham Pottery, and bred from long-standing Wrecclesham families (his mother was a Parratt), took himself a bride in 1925, he chose a young lady, Hilda Smith, from Cholsey, near Wallingford. On leaving school, Bertram started work at the Home and Colonial Stores at 6, West Street, Farnham, a company with which he would retain connection throughout his entire working life. His book, *Wrecclesham and District, Memories and Jottings*, was written when he was in his nineties. His sons, Norman and Derek, are actively researching their family tree and it is from them that several of the photographs have come which are in this volume.

Young George Hole, hair smarmed down with water for the special occasion of having a photograph taken, is seen here in the tiny back garden of his home in Middle Church Lane, about eighty years ago. One wonders what the lady, who is watching from the adjacent garden, is thinking.

George Collins was born in 1890 at Turner's Cottages, Wrecclesham, and started work as a garden boy at the Highlands, Shortheath. He had a very fine alto voice and was accepted as a chorister at Winchester Cathedral but was forced to give up this career when his father, a drayman with Farnham United Breweries, was killed near Clare Park, Crondall, by a runaway horse. This tragedy was recorded by George Sturt in his *Journals*. George joined the Northumberland Fusiliers in 1916, and this photograph, taken by Shrubbs, a Farnham photographer, records his first visit home to see his new son, Ronald George, who was born in February 1918. Young Ron grew up and, in the Second World War, served in the Royal Engineers from 1940-46, and was one of the soldiers to take part in the D-Day landings.

This picture appeared in the *Farnham Herald* with the following caption: 'Miss Mary Wells, daughter of Mr and Mrs W. Wells of Randall's Cottage, Dippenhall, who has been serving in the WRNS for two years, is now stationed at Malta on the Allied Forces Mediterranean staff. Prior to this NATO job she was at HMS *Victory*, Portsmouth. Formerly a member of the clerical staff of this newspaper, Miss Wells was a keen member of the Farnham Tower of Bell-ringers.' When she married she became the sister-in-law of young Ron, pictured above.

The Vanner family lived at Vanner's Farm, Wrecclesham, from 1660 until 1911 when James Vanner (seen standing outside the house on the main Farnham-Wrecclesham road) died. His eldest son, Reg, who was training to be a farmer, was only fourteen years old when his father died, so was unable to take over the farm and it was sold. The building became a guesthouse and, in 1968, the four Vanner children in this photograph, Daisy, Reginald, Richard and Rosamund (seen on page 11 outside their childhood home, together with their younger brother, Patrick) returned to it for one night of nostalgia. It was the first time in fifty years that they had all been together again.

Superintendent Simmonds (left) was a much-loved police officer in Farnham who, for many years, before moving into a detached house in Firgrove Hill, lived with his family above the old police station in Union Road, adjacent to Church House. Here he is pictured with his young grandson and granddaughter. It must be presumed that the policeman on the right is a visiting officer of some note (and kindness) to have himself photographed so informally outside the police station.

Members of the family of Superintendent Simmonds, pictured around 1920 at the recently installed fountain in Gostrey Meadow. The fountain, although not working, is still *in situ*. The snapshot was taken by another member of Supt Simmonds' family, Evelyn, always known as Jo, Farnham's first female photographer to be in business in the town.

Young Arthur Slaught, whose father was killed in the final hours of the First World War, salutes the memorial in Gostrey Meadow, just after it was unveiled on 10 April 1921 bearing the names of 278 Farnham men who had lost their lives. Because his father died when he was so young he was 'adopted' by the Farnham police as their mascot – his grandfather was the police superintendent at the station.

The very attractive Hilda Hole, related to the young George featured earlier, had this studio portrait taken when she was in service in Castle Street. Hilda eventually married Jack Sparrow, had two children, Basil and Joan, and lived in Roman Way until she died.

Toy cars were extremely novel in the early 1920s, when the young granddaughter of Farnham's Police Superintendent Simmonds peddled her way across Gostrey Meadow in the early 1920s. How fashionable she must have felt with such a large feather in her hat.

William Wells was born in Beaver's Close on 3 January 1897. He was apprenticed as a carpenter to Mardon and Ball and, during the First World War, served in the Hampshire Yeomanry. He later transferred to the Royal Hampshire Regiment and saw service in France, Italy and Belgium. After demobilization in 1919, he returned to Mardon and Ball. As a foreman carpenter he worked on most of the large houses in the Farnham area but, as was the custom at that time, he spent many weeks (Monday to Saturday) in the winter 'living in' seaside hotels while renovating them, often working as far away as Brighton and Hastings. He lived his entire life in the Dora's Green/Dippenhall area and, still in good health, celebrated his 100th birthday in January 1997, as seen above right, with a telegram from the Queen.

Two
Health and Welfare

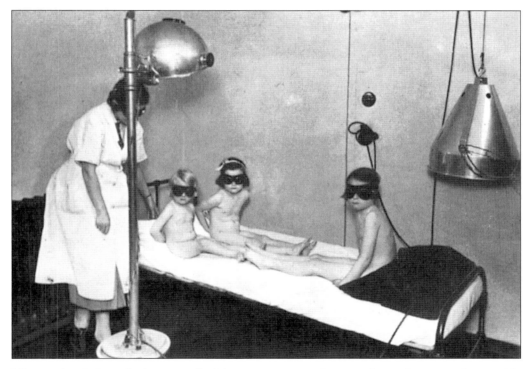

Ultra-violet light, which was called 'sunray treatment', was often administered to sickly children in the 1940s and early 1950s. Initially this treatment, in Farnham, was believed to have been given at Brightwells Clinic but by 1950 the Curative Post, as it was known, was operating from the physiotherapy department at Farnham Hospital, Hale Road. Children wore goggles, but nothing else, whilst receiving the treatment.

In November 1945, Mary McIlvenna, a young Irish girl, left her country and came to England to become a nurse at Farnham Hospital. Several more young Irish girls came here, too, which is why the list of nurses in this picture has a distinctive Irish feel about it. Some of the girls remained here, marrying Englishmen, and it was Mary who managed to name everyone on this photograph, which belongs to Don Banks, son of Mr Banks, the former workhouse master, who is seated in the front row. Although the photograph has been damaged, its rarity justifies its inclusion here. Farnham Infirmary (later Hospital) was adjacent to the workhouse. The line-up is, from left to right, back row: Nurses A. McQuade, K. McQuade, N. Truckle, J. Dexter, H. McKenna, A. O'Leary, U. O'Leary, M.T. McIlvenna, J. Hern, E. Harker, F. Smith, N. Tansey, M. Mulholland, A. Kiernan, B. Butcher, N. Tomlin, G. Bunce, N.R. Finlay. Middle row: Nurses N. Higgins, P. Callen, N. Jackson, N. Plestor, N. Beatty, K. Marchant, I. Pullen, Sisters Warrior, Foden, Simpson, Saunders, Hunt, Nurses S. Hole, N. Northcott, M.N. Egan, N. Jemson, N. Abrahamson. Front row: Nurses A. Heather, N. Brislane, Sister King, Mr Banks, Sister Doherty, Dr K. Roberts, Home Sister Mason, Dr Bedo Hobbs, Matron Miss Nicholls, Dr Gordon Roberts, Assistant Matron Miss Hunt, Dr Herman, Sisters Doyle and Connors, Nurse N. Anderson. The staff are sitting in front of the main entrance to the old Farnham Hospital.

This building, Farnham Hospital, which had 184 beds and a resident medical staff, an outpatient department and all ancillary services as well as an accident and emergency unit, is due for demolition in 2002/03. Therefore, this photograph, from around 1948, will be of particular interest to the hundreds of thousands of people who have been nursed there since it was built in 1900. Mary Ward, which was situated on the first floor of the building, to the right of the main entrance, was also the place where hundreds of Farnham babies were born. On the first floor, to the left of the entrance, was the women's surgical ward.

South of the town, in the area to the rear of the present Weydon school and Bardsley Drive Estate, once stood the Farnham Isolation Hospital, or Green Lane Hospital as it was usually called, which had around fifty beds. It was built in 1898 at a cost of £7,750, when it had twenty beds and two cots. In 1909 it was enlarged, at a further cost of £800. When isolation for infectious diseases, such as diphtheria, was no longer as necessary as it had formerly been, the hospital was demolished. This happened about forty years ago, in favour of housing. In his memoirs, Bertram Elkins says that he remembers 'the grounds being surrounded by a corrugated-iron fence with a saw-tooth top edge to prevent intrusion'. This photograph shows the hospital's cubicle block.

In 1939 a block of seven bungalows, interconnected by corridors and with a central dining hall and modern kitchen, was opened for old folk in the grounds of Farnham Hospital. It was built by the local firm of Crosby & Co. Ltd. At that time these homes were considered to be the best in Surrey, and possibly in the whole country. Another block was added in the early 1950s. The complex was demolished in the late 1990s to make way for housing. The demolition contractor asked £50 for each of the original rainwater heads, with 1939 embossed on them, from the original St James's Home buildings.

Trimmer's Hospital, Menin Way (now the Phyllis Tuckwell Hospice), was opened on 31 July 1935 by HRH Lady Patricia Ramsay. It cost a total of £16,500. Then it looked out on to open fields but within four years, Farnham Girls' Grammar School was built next door. This was completed in 1939 and the girls moved from a cramped building in West Street to a large unit with vast grounds, adjacent to the hospital (which had also moved, from limited space in East Street, four years earlier).

During the Second World War and for some time afterwards, a day nursery, for thirty children, was held in East Street, at the old Trimmer's Hospital site situated to the right of the footpath into Stoke Hills. It is interesting to see that some of the children have wooden hoops with which to play, a toy more usually seen in Victorian photographs.

Dr Caldicot was a much-loved, if somewhat severe, doctor of the 'old school', who had such presence that his female patients in Rowledge and Wrecclesham almost curtseyed to him if they chanced to pass him in the street. Here he is about to enter his car on his last morning in practice before his retirement.

Where Boots the Chemist now stands, at 49 The Borough, Timothy White's 'Cash Chemists' once operated. Not only were prescriptions dispensed but household goods, such as galvanized zinc baths and buckets, were also sold. A chemist appears to have been operating from this spot for at least 150 years, from William Portello in the mid-nineteenth century through to William Higgins, Louis Cullingford, and Timothy White's until the last quarter of the twentieth century when Boots moved there from their smaller unit at 41/42 The Borough.

Three
Mobile
Communications

The Fox and the Happy Home could not have been much closer, and both public houses were under the same Courage brewery. Here, the No. 16, Aldershot and District Traction Company (ADTC) bus can be seen on its way into Farnham. This scene was photographed around 1968.

A wheelbarrow is hardly what one might expect in a chapter entitled 'Mobile Communications' but for the gardener wheeling his manure along Thomas's Hill Road (just off the Ridgway junction), the barrow was easier than carrying 'muck' by the forkful.

H. Corps had branches in both East Street and Downing Street. The frontage, above, was at approximately where the entrance to the office of HM Inspector of Taxes is today, in what is now known as The Woolmead. All types of leather goods were sold and repaired, including horse harnesses, bags and portmanteaux – bags which were used to carry clothing on journeys. The word 'portmanteau' means, literally, a cloak or mantle carrier, and was in everyday use until the 1920s, but today is scarcely ever heard.

Almost forty years ago Beryl Pring was the lollipop lady by The Fox, at The Bourne. She was 'manning' her crossing patrol site when the photographer arrived. The mother and children were hurrying, so no waiting for the photographer, hence this slightly blurred picture. When lollipop signs were first introduced a popular joke of the day was to ask how it could act as a contraceptive and 'stop children?'

At first glance this view down East Street, looking west, appears to be the same as at present. However, the buildings in the centre on the left are no more. They were demolished to make way for the Dogflud loop road. The double-fronted white building towards the back, left, is the Kar Ling Kwong restaurant, which is still there today. The centre building, with a down-pipe which is clearly visible, was once a youth centre named Nowhere, arranged and organized by the late Sir John Verney, author, artist and councillor, to cater for the young people who said they 'Had nowhere to go.'

The question of a flyover, underpass or bridge at Hickley's Corner has been under discussion for well over forty years. This photograph shows a model of one of the designs for an underpass which was put forward in 1969 as a proposal to ease traffic congestion and to help save lives at this notorious junction. The large building at the road junction is that of Hickley's ironmonger's shop, from which the junction derives its name. To the left of the building is Abbey Street and the large building in the foreground has been known as The Railway Arms, The Railway Hotel, The Blue Boy and ,currently, The Exchange.

Crosby Doors, which operated from the old Lion Brewery site in West Street, began to specialize in door manufacture after the Second World War. They soon expanded and had branches and subsidiary companies in Swindon and Somerset as well as Farnham. Its head office address was given as Craven House, West Street, a unit over a quarter-mile away from the factory site where these lorries were lined up in 1972.

Those people who remember 'Miss Margaret' (Mrs Margaret Wenham) as a stooping, always well-dressed lady who was never seen around the town without at least one shopping bag, might find difficulty in realizing that she is the same person as the little girl pictured in this toy aeroplane around 1926 when, as Margaret Squires, she would have been about four years old.

Horse-drawn milk carts and milk delivery boys on bicycles stretched right across Castle Street for this photograph of around 1910. The Farnham Dairy Company, 12 West Street, owners of the horses and carts, advertised that 'all utensils [were] cleaned by steam apparatus' and that their high-class milk, butter and cream came from its own farms.

This line-up of Ford Zephyr cars was photographed in the 1960s by Jim Bodkin, of Dockenfield. It was taken outside the works of E.D. Abbott, close to the railway arch at Wrecclesham. Abbott's converted Ford saloon cars into estate vehicles. These became so popular that the hitherto coach-building work and vehicle servicing for which Abbott's was renowned began to be neglected. However, the Ford motor company soon noticed the popularity of the conversions, executed at Wrecclesham, and began to produce their own designs, thus spelling the death knell for the Abbott conversions. Soon afterwards the garage closed down and almost all of its records were destroyed.

Once upon a time buses from at least three local companies used to transport local people about. This photograph was taken in 1927, in South Street, and shows the Aldershot and District Company's No. 10 bus, which terminated at Shortheath, being driven towards the railway station. On the left can be seen the Bush Tap and in the background one can just glimpse W. Gratrick, saddler, next to J.H. Wilcox, the gents' outfitter, which was founded in 1883.

Nash's Bakery, at Folly Hill, Hale, pulled out all the stops to put on this float at a local carnival with Lloyd Loom chairs, wooden trellis and lots of balloons, plus six bakers and two small girls in fancy dress. The vehicle in front is presumably representing the Co-operative Stores in Farnham, because a notice in the back of the van shows that it is advertising C.W.S (Co-operative Wholesale Society) strawberry jam.

For almost 100 years there has been a Swain and Jones garage in East Street. Until the 1930s petrol was dispensed in the way that can be seen, above, with a man in attendance. The present Swain and Jones showroom, on the south side of East Street, is on the same site as seen in this photograph.

This line-up of fire engines, ancient and more recent, was arranged in South Street, where there was once a fire station in part of what is now the Locality Office and Tourist Information Centre.

Four

Drop Me a Line

Castle Steps, Farnham.

In 1911 at least one hop garden in Farnham ended its picking on 6 September. The message on the back of this Valentine's Series postcard tells the addressee that the sender is hop picking and that 'We finish tomorrow and have a supper and a singsong'. Hops, still on poles, can be seen on the left of the view, and on the right, children are standing on the steps, which are set at intervals of seven steps and seven strides so that a blind bishop who once lived at Farnham Castle could get to and from it unaided.

Hammondswood is one of the very large houses in the Rowledge/Wrecclesham area. This picture was taken and published by J.H. Dodman of Frensham. In these two villages there were perhaps a dozen large houses which gave work to several hundred men and women who lived in tiny cottages. At the beginning of the twentieth century, when the population of Rowledge was about 600, there was nothing in between the very large and the very small by way of private accommodation in this spot on the Hampshire/Surrey border.

One might expect that the Manor House would be the largest of the houses in a village but, as can be seen in this postcard, in Frensham this was clearly not the case – although, to be fair, the building above is of far greater antiquity than the 'big' houses. Although undated, the postcard was published by R. Sturt & Son, Frensham, and the photographer was G.E. Langrish.

One of the very interesting points to be observed in postcards of the Edwardian era is the high number which, like this one, were printed in a dot format (the technique known as screen printing). Mr Porter, at his small shop in the village square, probably sold the stamp as well as this postcard when it was sent with a Rowledge postmark, on 8 November 1905, to Mr Ron West, The Alpines, South View, Farnham.

Despite the isolation of Frensham School and the ample open ground around it, it somehow seems incongruous to see a football goalpost on the grass to the right of the school. Could there really have been enough boys, when this card was sent from Frensham on 28 December 1907, to make up two football teams in order that a game could be played? Frensham school is one of the oldest schools in the Farnham area and still proudly owns many of the logbooks from the nineteenth century.

Manley Bridge, Rowledge, in 1913, a postcard made from a photograph taken by A. Brown. This was once the only route out of the village to Farnham until Mr Fuller, who owned a house on the site of the present Frensham Heights school, wanted to get his coach on to the Turnpike Road (as the present A325 was then called); he laid the foundations of the road which now bears his name, although originally it was called the Coach Road.

Bearing a Frensham, Farnham, postmark and an indecipherable date in July 1916 (two years into the First World War) this postcard was published by Sturt, Frensham, and printed in England. It depicts the cauldron which folklore decrees was loaned by Mother Ludlam, from Moor Park, to a person who did not return it by the due date. Mother Ludlam is said to have chased the offender, who took refuge, with the cauldron, in Frensham church, where it has remained ever since. The message on the back of the postcard reads 'Cream arrived safely. Thank you very much.'

These two postcards, one unfranked, the other posted at Frensham on 20 June 1907, both show views of Shortfield, Frensham. F. Elderfield took the Shortfield Common picture (above) published by R. Sturt & Son, Frensham, and Inge & Co., Haslemere, was responsible for the misty scene across the Green (below). Both views would be instantly recognizable today, almost a century later; sometimes it seems as if time has passed Shortfield by.

Bearing the postmark of Frensham and posted on 14 September 1905, this view of Pierrepont House was published by R. Sturt & Son, Frensham, and as Mr Sturt was an excellent photographer, he probably took the photograph as well. This 'north front' view has changed very little over the past ninety-seven years. When Eli and Hermina (Emma) Nash, for twenty-three years workers on the Pierrepont Estate, celebrated their golden wedding anniversary in 1910, their employers, Mr Richard and The Lady Constance Combe, held a party for the couple on the lawn seen above, and presented the pair with a silver mounted biscuit barrel.

The wooden footbridge at Pierrepont, Frensham, as photographed by G.E. Langrish and published by R. Sturt & Son, Frensham in around 1909. The postal charge, set in a block on which a stamp could be affixed, was one-halfpenny 'inland' and one penny 'foreign.' Pierrepont House, adjacent to this view, was for many years the home of the wealthy Combe family. More recently the building was a school and now it houses the Ellel Christian Mission.

Five
The Famous

Screaming 'Lord' (David) Sutch may have annoyed conventional politicians when he stood as a candidate for the Raving Loony Party at elections, but he was an extremely caring man who raised vast sums for charity. When he visited The Castle public house, in Crondall, he continued to raise funds for charity until well after midnight. Neither 'Lord' Sutch nor The Castle remain – the would-be politician has died and the hostelry has been converted into a house.

Farnham has had a number of national sporting personalities including Mike Hawthorn (motor racing), William 'Billy' Beldham (cricket), Neil 'Boy' McCormick (boxing), Richard 'Dick' Vanner (football) and, currently, Graham Thorpe. Graham, the youngest of three sporting brothers from Wrecclesham, has captained England in many Test matches and has also played football for England. He first came to the notice of the public when he was eleven and captained the Surrey Under-11s in three cricket matches, all of which Surrey won. He learned his football with the Wrecclesham Cub Scouts. An article in the *Surrey and Hants News* in September 1980 ended: 'The future in sport holds a lot for all three brothers and with the right application and dedication maybe all three (Ian, Alan and Graham) will fulfil their sporting ambitions.' They have.

Vera Lynn, the 'Forces' Sweetheart', was a regular visitor to Farnham throughout her childhood and teenage years – her aunt lived near the crossroads at Weybourne. Vera bought sweets in the late Vi Mason's shop (now a hairdresser's) and wrote with affection about Weybourne in her autobiography. She continued, for many years, to make visits to the town, staying at The Bush with her husband and daughter. Here she is signing one of her books in Hammicks Bookshop in Lion and Lamb Yard.

Field Marshal Viscount Montgomery of Alamein was once the district's most famous resident. In the summer of 1981 a definitive biography of the wartime army leader was published and, as advance notice of this book, the *Surrey and Hants News* published this photograph of him, taken about twenty years earlier, showing the old soldier discussing a vehicle he was about to buy from the Tourist Trophy Garage in East Street. With the Field Marshal (right) are Mr J.H. Adams and Mr Don Scott (centre).

41

Bill Wallis, who lived in Hale Road as a youngster, first attended East Street (later Park) School, moving on to the Farnham Grammar School where he later became head boy before winning a scholarship to Cambridge. He was a journalist on the *Surrey and Hants News*, later taking up a career on the stage. He was in *Beyond The Fringe* in the West End, and later played Harold Wilson in *Mrs Wilson's Diary* at the Criterion Theatre, in London. He has also performed in a number of Shakespearean plays and has played many other parts, including comedy roles in *Black Adder*. He now lives in Bath.

Arthur English, the original 'spiv' of the 1950s, lived in Aldershot, just over the Hampshire/Surrey border, but spent many hours on charitable works in Farnham, particularly at the Kar Ling Kwong restaurant in East Street, where this photograph was taken. Arthur, as well as being a comedian, was an amateur artist and one of his paintings, of a clown, was auctioned at a fund-raising event in the restaurant in aid of the Phyllis Tuckwell Hospice.

Liza Goddard, actress and former wife of rock singer Alvin Stardust, appeared in *1066 And All That* when she was at Farnham Girls' Grammar School. When she was the subject of BBC's *This Is Your Life* programme in January 1984, she came face-to-face with a former teacher, eighty-one-year-old Miss Mary Eggar, who said of that school production, 'We little thought in *1066* that we had a star who was going to shine on into 1984.' Miss Eggar died, aged 100, in October 2002.

Loyd Grossman, the well-known television personality, visited the Museum of Farnham with South West Surrey MP Virginia Bottomley, and was met by a number of children from the Saturday Museum Club. They posed with the famous guests on the staircase of the Grade I listed Georgian building, which has a number of chimneys, although these had not been swept by the young sweep, Lindsey Macvean, seen here next to the famous chef.

The BBC television programme, *What's My Line* ran for many years and was a great favourite with many people. For a considerable time the question master was Richard Dimbleby, who lived at Haslemere, and he can be seen in this picture from when the team visited the Memorial Hall, Farnham, in the mid-1960s.

Many films and television programmes have been shot on location at Frensham Pond. Here, Bill Simpson, Dr Finlay of *Dr Finlay's Casebook*, is seen fishing at the edge of a 'Scottish' lake in Surrey.

A number of famous people were regular customers at the Gulshan restaurant, Heath End, in the mid-1980s, when Noor Ali owned the business. Bruce Forsyth and Russ Abbot sometimes came together, and here the performers, owner and staff were snapped one evening by a local journalist who was in the restaurant at the time enjoying an Indian meal.

Six

The Not-So-Famous

In their obituary in the *Farnham Herald*, in the spring of 2002, Monica Jones wrote, 'Margaret and Matthew Wenham, who died a fortnight apart, achieved a place in the Farnham legend and were, themselves, the stuff of which legends are made.' Matthew, like his father before him, was a rag-and-bone man. His wife, daughter of a military officer, was always immaculately dressed in a two-piece costume and hat and was affectionately known to almost everyone as 'Miss Margaret,' despite the fact that she had been married to Matt for more than thirty-five years. Margaret was extremely generous to staff in the shops, banks and cafés which she frequented and she had a particular fondness for children. With their passing Farnham lost two of its few remaining 'characters.'

Harold Cole, grandson of Eli and Emma Nash who worked on the Pierrepont estate, worked for the *Farnham Herald* for sixty-four years, rising from the office boy, as seen here, to a director of the company. Widely travelled by land, sea and air (including the first Concorde flight to America), he was an ardent royalist and a letter from the late Queen Elizabeth the Queen Mother was read at his funeral.

Angela Bradford Pullen, a Miss Farnham of the 1970s, chats to a child at a local playgroup, quite happy that the attention is on a rag doll rather than on herself.

In the last quarter of the twentieth century Stella and Ray Perry, from Sunnydell Lane, probably did more than any other couple in Farnham to care for injured birds and beasts, and they did it free of charge. Only ill-health eventually stopped them from their charitable work which was known and respected over a wide area. Stella's father was a potter at Wrecclesham Pottery throughout his life.

In 1965 three men came up with a plan to row the Atlantic. David Johnstone, left, a Farnham journalist who lived at Crondall, had the idea while drinking in the Bush Hotel. He planned to make the trip with Richard Brooks, right, who had been a producer at the Castle Theatre, Farnham, and John Hoare, centre, from Leicester, who had answered an advertisement that David had put in *The Times*. In the event Richard Brooks did not take part. He emigrated to Australia, where he still lives. David, thirty-four, and John, twenty-nine, left the American coast in their specially built boat, the *Puffin*, in May 1966. They rowed for 106 days before being swamped by Hurricane Faith. *Puffin* was found, upside-down and empty, on 14 October. It was 800 miles south east of St John's, Newfoundland.

Florence Nightingale, the best-known nurse in British history, was a frequent visitor to Farnham, both to Waverley Abbey House and to Lowlands (now Brightwells). Her goddaughter, Florence Paget, who ran a successful antiques business in The Borough, known as The Spinning Wheel (now Bewley's), is believed to have told Florence Nightingale about the new hospital in Farnham which was completed on 14 May 1900, and the great nurse gave a silver communion set for the benefit of the sick patients and the staff there. In April 2002, the gift was 'presented' to the hospital once again, during the AGM of the League of Friends of Farnham Hospital. It was used again on Whit Sunday 2002, exactly 100 years after the set was originally donated. Hannah Wilson, a pupil at South Farnham school, chose Florence Nightingale as a Victorian profile project and is pictured here, in 2002, with the set.

Madge and Henry Jackson spent half a lifetime collecting old agricultural implements and putting them on display in fields adjacent to their home at Tilford. It was originally known as the Old Kiln Museum but now that it has expanded to include buildings (which have been dismantled at various sites and re-erected at the museum) it is called the Rural Life Centre.

Jack Hardingham, right, is one of the last two members of the Hardingham family to still live in Farnham. At one time Freddie Hardingham, his uncle, was a collector of antiques and a master carpenter here. Another of Jack's uncles, Arthur Hardingham, ran an antiques business in East Street, and his Auntie Gladys ran a second-hand book shop in West Street. Jack has interests in all three subjects, woodwork, antiques and old books.

These Stan Laurel and Oliver Hardy lookalikes, Jean Parratt, left, and Maureen Gates, as they appeared in a mid-1980s Farnham Carnival. As a result of this annual event the Farnham Lions, the organizers, raise thousands of pounds for charity each year.

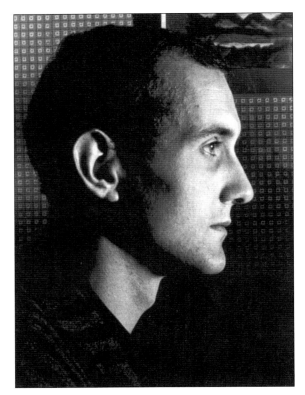

Michael Beby, who lived in both Hale Road and Stephendale Road, Farnham, became known in the gossip columns of the national newspapers in the 1960s as 'the prince of the beatniks'. He announced, at the age of eighteen, that he would never work again, and he never has. Instead he had a series of very rich and pretty girlfriends with whom he travelled the world. They included Carola Casson, the daughter of Sir Hugh Casson, and Henrietta Guinness. However, he never married and now lives alone in a small flat in Bath.

For more than forty years, from 1950, the *Surrey and Hants News* office was situated in West Street. Outside its office, the town's two traffic wardens are posed wearing their new uniforms. Karen Skinner, left, and Judith Briggs look happy despite the town's traffic problems. Judith is represented, life-size, in the Transport Room at the Museum of Farnham.

Always with a smile or a kind word, Annie Martin was probably Farnham's best-known woman for almost sixty years, after coming here during the Second World War. Annie started the family greengrocery business at the bottom of Castle Street and was never happier than when she was selling strawberries there. She had an old clothes boiler, in which she cooked the beetroot, in the yard behind her house in Long Garden Walk, a task she continued up to the time she died. Farnham literally stood still for her funeral, in tribute to one of the few remaining real characters of the town.

Christopher Monk, from Churt, was a retired schoolteacher who gave up teaching history to make, repair and play serpents, one of which he is holding in this photograph. In a newspaper article in 1987, Mr Monk said that Wagner, Beethoven and Mendelssohn had all composed for the instrument, which was first devised in the sixteenth century.

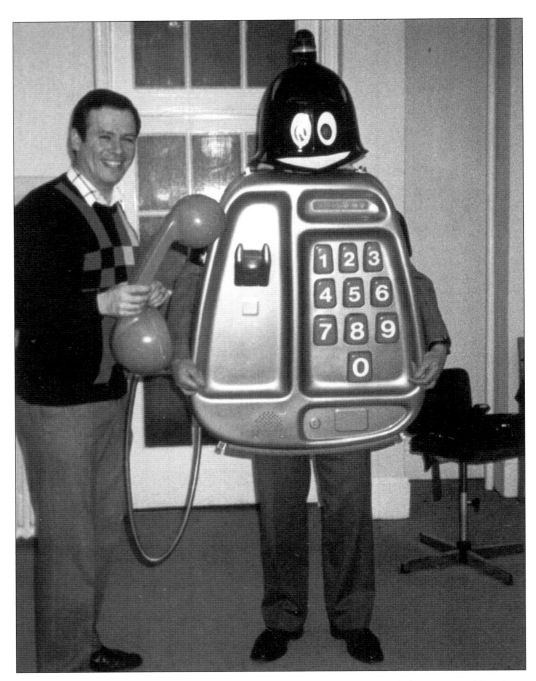

An outsize telephone topped by a policeman's helmet was seen around the streets of Farnham in the spring of 1988. As part of Farnham police's Crime Prevention Week British Telecom loaned the telephone robot to the police in an attempt to get youngsters to stop vandalising telephone boxes. PC Patrick Webber, a friendly and genial constable, arranged a crime prevention demonstration in an empty shop on West Street and is pictured here with his robotic friend.

Seven
Cheers!

In the 1990s many public houses, which had served the needs of local people for around 150 years, became the targets of property developers. Brewers, interested in making a quick profit on the land rather than a slower one on selling beer, sold the hostelries for housing purposes. The Halfway House, Farnborough Road, Heath End, suffered this fate. Charlie Wenham, the town's most famous rag-and-bone merchant (and father of Matthew, mentioned earlier) used to have a yard opposite this pub. In his younger days Charlie once took the prize for the best turned-out soldier on parade.

Watney Combe Reid & Co. Ltd.

(Close to Capital & Counties Bank)

CASTLE STREET

Telephone :
41 Farnham

FARNHAM, SURREY

ALE & STOUT SUPPLIED IN CASK & BOTTLE

WINES & SPIRITS OF THE BEST QUALITY ALWAYS IN STOCK

Price Lists on Application   -::-   Delivery to all parts

G. E. ALDRIDGE, Manager

Although Watney, Combe, Reid and Co. Ltd, formed in 1898, left Farnham many years ago, traces of the firm can still be seen in Farnham. On close examination the company name, seen in the advertisement above, can still be discerned behind the present St Georges Yard sign on the bar, across the entrance to what is now a house and office complex. The Capital & Counties Bank, given as a site indication in the advertisement, later became Lloyd's Bank (still *in situ*). Mr Reid lived in Farnham and Mr Combe's home was at Pierrepont, Frensham, so the owners probably kept a very close eye on their brewery's depot. This advertisement appeared in *The Borough Guide to Farnham*, published just before the First World War began in 1914.

A mile or so from the western town boundary of Farnham stands the Bull Inn, on a mound to prevent it from being flooded, as the River Wey regularly floods the surrounding fields. Situated on the Farnham-Alton Road, it has changed little over several centuries, apart from the breweries whose liveries it has carried. Today it is a free house owned and run by Robert Lewis and Grant Edmead. In the 1980s and early 1990s Grant was a partner in a video shop in South Street, Farnham.

Inside the Coach and Horses, Castle Street, in the late 1960s. Rodney Hinton, left, became the youngest councillor on the old Farnham Urban District Council in 1966, when he won a seat for Labour in the Castle Ward at the age of twenty-three. This made him doubly unusual – his youth and the fact that he was a socialist. Mike Weeks is on Rodney's left, then Tom Underwood and author Guy Bellamy, whose first novel, *The Secret Lemonade Drinker*, was partly set in this hostelry.

Posted on 13 September 1911, this picture of the Hare and Hounds, The Square, Rowledge, shows that although the village did not yet have electricity (which reached there in 1912), a motor car could be hired at this hostelry, there was good accommodation for cyclists and travellers, trains arriving at Farnham could be met and, in the centre of the road outside the pub, was one of the village's seven oil-burning street lamps, which had been installed in 1901.

Set in the valley adjacent to the stream along which barrels of beer were floated from the bridge at the bottom of Sandrock Hill stands the Bat and Ball. Once a hop grower's home, the beerhouse grew from the owner's habit of keeping back a few pennies of his workers' wages in order that they could have beer at the end of the week's toil. It had a beerhouse licence in 1865. Parts of the building, which is currently under threat of demolition (2002), in order for houses to be built upon the site, are around 300 years old.

Frank 'Punch' Parratt, left, drank in the Bat and Ball every day the pub was open for sixty-four years. He had his own corner and bar stool and for the past fifteen years there has been a plaque in his memory on the wall. Known to everyone as 'Punch,' he was a master plasterer by trade, and built his own bungalow, 'Cascade', near to the pub. The occasion for which he is seen behind the bar is an ownership takeover early in the 1980s, when Johnny 'Boy-Boy' Martin became the new owner of the Bat and Ball.

The Hop Blossom public house, in Long Garden Walk, had its first alehouse licence in 1864. When this photograph was taken the hostelry licence was held by Catherine Clark. Over the years the Hop Blossom has attracted some interesting licensees. As a free house in the late 1970s and early 1980s, the man in charge was Tony Brown, whose application to renew his licence was refused by the magistrates – this made local newspaper headlines. In the late 1990s, under Fuller, Smith and Turner, Stephen Brewitt was evicted, but not before, once again, newspaper, radio and television coverage.

The Castle had an alehouse licence from at least 1859. In 1904 it was stated that it 'provided bread, cheese, teas and minerals and had accommodation for two persons and six horses.' In February 1983, Colin Hicks, brother of rock 'n' roll star Tommy Steele, became its landlord, but left suddenly in November 1984. Its days as an inn were almost at an end and, although alcohol is still dispensed there, it is only as 'off-sales' at a twenty-four-hour 'convenience' store.

The Borough, Farnham, before the First World War. Above the ground-floor level, little has changed on any of these buildings over the last ninety years. The Ship sign has gone and the lower part of the building has been changed. The balcony on The Bush has also been removed. Apart from these small points, and the fact that a man is riding a bicycle on the road when it was still two-way traffic, this is another of the instantly recognizable postcard views of this town. Written at the entrance to The Ship are the words, 'Stabling to let, Dinners, Teas and Billiards'.

In the early years of the twentieth century, Farnham United Breweries, based in West Street, Farnham, had agencies as far away as Winchester. Bottles of wine and beer, as well as barrels of the latter, were delivered by a man with a horse and cart, and when both needed a rest, the cart and its contents had to be parked in a shady spot under a tree.

Until the mid-1960s, Downing Street was frequently flooded when the River Wey burst its banks, as can be seen above. This was an inn, known by at least four names, including The Hop Bag, which was closed in 1987 after a murder was committed outside the establishment. The yard behind the building, adjacent to the central car park, is said to be haunted.

Eight
The Younger Generation

During the early 1970s Park School, in Hale Road, had its own radio station known as Radio Park. It was organized by Pete Wisbey, a BBC employee, and every Friday afternoon the children would listen to the programme which they had produced themselves. Outside broadcasts were included and this photograph was taken in the garden of John Noakes, a *Blue Peter* presenter, who, at that time, lived just outside Farnham. Pete's two sons, Piers and Duncan, are pictured here with Jamie Rose, left, Maria Clark and John.

In the Nativity Play at the Bourne School, around 1975, Lisa Beagley is holding the baby Jesus (also known as a Tiny Tears doll, which was a very popular request from Santa at that time). Thomas Hall, right, is the only one of the curtain-cloaked Wise Men whose identity is known.

The traditional school 'long photograph' was taken at the smaller, private schools as well as the grammar schools in the town, and here, complete with its school logo of England's patron saint, are the pupils and staff of St George's School, Castle Street, in 1951. On the complete

Although this photograph of adults may seem out of place in a chapter entitled 'The Younger Generation' it is quite acceptable because it shows, second from right, Paul French, the new, young headmaster at Farnham Grammar School at a school prize-giving in the early 1970s. Paul French later saw the amalgamation of the town's two grammar schools, one for each sex, into the Farnham Sixth Form College.

photograph ninety-eight children can be seen but unfortunately, because of its width, only ninety appear here. After leaving Castle Street the school moved to Pierrepont House, Frensham, and later became an integrated part of Frensham Heights School.

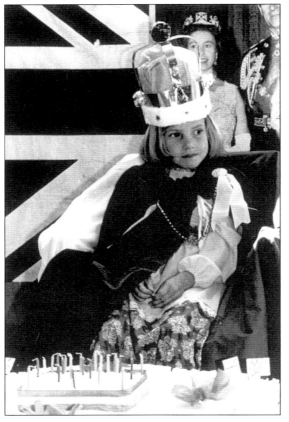

Bourne Guides in fancy dress in the mid-1960s at St Martin's church hall, Lower Bourne. Fancy-dress hire shops had not reached this area at that time so the girls, and their parents, used their imagination and inventiveness to make their own garments, including a Fuchsia Flower, Oranges and Lemons, Robin Hood and Autumn (covered in an assortment of real leaves stuck on brown paper).

The cake in front of the 'queen' was made in sections, each teacher at the Bourne School making a square cake each before they were put together as a whole and then iced and decorated. Michelle Raymont – the 'Queen' – is seen here at the school's Silver Jubilee celebrations in 1977.

Pupils at St Christopher's School, in 1953, photographed in Brightwells Gardens. At that time their school was in rooms at the United Reformed church in South Street. From left to right, back row: Diana Wories, Susan Boswell, Jonathan Drapers, Mary-Ann Marshall, Geoffrey Stratford, David Marshall, Carol Croly, Tristan Rees-Roberts, Philip Pendarves, Sandra Moses, Guy Pope, Mark Doughty, Carina Campbell. Second row: Ivor Galen, Ian Elliott, Sally Buckingham, Peter Moss, Mary Wedgwood, Martin Underdown, Thea Baily, John Aldred, Malcolm Spalding, Alistair Hunt, Helen Knight, Theresa Howard. Third row: Edward Thomas, Paul (?) Mawsey, Clare Elliott, Mrs Hickey, Mrs Whistler, Gillian Hunt, Mrs Vincent, -?-, Peggy Coutu, Jennifer Hume, Jennet Baily, John Cable. Front row: Brian Johnson, Nicola Hobson, David Duvall, Richard Thomas, Richard Winter, Billy Buckingham, Jane Wories.

Farnham has always had strong links with the Scout movement since its founder, Robert Baden-Powell, moved to Pax Hill, Bentley, almost a century ago. Here, on the stage at the Bourne, taking part in a Gang Show, are the Bourne Cubs, with Richard Martin third from left.

Showing off the puppets which were on sale at the Bourne Guides Autumn Fair in 1966 are, amongst others, Pat Young, Lorna Huckle and Beverlie Martin. At one time the Hon. Wendy Baden-Powell, granddaughter of the founders of the Scout and Guide movements – Robert and Olave Baden-Powell – was a member of the Bourne Guides under Miss Gladys Farmer, who was her captain.

The boys at East Street Elementary School (later to be known as Park School) pictured in 1907 after a successful competition for the swimming shield and trophies. A list of the races which the boys had won is written in chalk on the blackboard beneath the name of their school and the date.

Posed outside Badshot Lea School in the mid-1930s, these boys and girls were almost all children of village residents who made their living from the land, usually working for a farmer such as Mr Tice. The children at this school were unusual inasmuch as they had a good grounding in archaeology. Mr W. Rankine, the head, was an amateur archaeologist of some repute and it was he who initially discovered the Mesolithic site close to the present Six Bells roundabout.

Weydon School's Youth Orchestra open evening, around 1975, where Christopher Weeks is in the music room playing on the French horn. Lyn Summerbell is fourth from left.

Liverpool Building Society, East Street, held a painting competition in 1975 and the winners were invited for a photograph call. Included here are Katharine Martin, Jonathan Powell and Samantha Pollard, the latter front row, fourth from left, who was the winner in the younger age group and received a cheque for £10. Traffic was still going in both directions in the street at that time, as can be seen by sections of cars through the windows on both sides of the screen on which the pictures are exhibited.

Young Agnes Tubb, with her doll, in about 1925. She attended St Andrew's School and, after leaving at fourteen, the statutory school-leaving age in those days, she went to work in a ladies' fashion shop in the town.

One of the last photographs taken of children at play in Park School, Hale Road, before it closed in July 1986. The two school buildings remain on the site (the smaller one having been used for a television series, *The Grafters*, in the late 1990s). The larger was a social services centre for a number of years but both buildings are empty once again, despite the attempts by Barratt Homes to obtain permission to demolish them and build houses there. Local residents have campaigned for years to retain the buildings and hope that a scene such as the one above could one day be a regular sight there again.

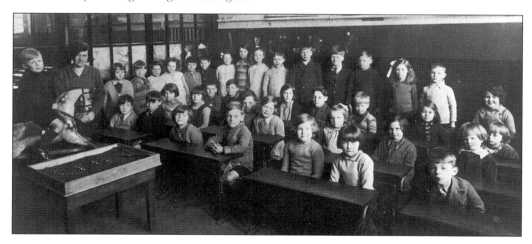

A classroom of thirty-nine boys and girls at the Bourne School in 1932. Their teacher was Miss Mills, and young Eddie Trusler must have done some really good work to have been given the honour of sitting astride the rocking horse while the class photograph was taken. Eddie Trusler was to become a photographer when he grew up and it was he who took the picture of his daughter, Rosalind, on page 75.

Here Boy Scouts are seen marching along Union Road to St Andrew's parish church. The larger of the two buildings behind them is the former Co-operative Society's shop, part of which had earlier been a Nonconformist chapel and the words of the Lord's Prayer, although painted over, could still be seen on the wall above the cash desk in the carpet department. The building on the left is part of the former Hop Bag public house.

Robert Baden-Powell, founder of the Boy Scout movement, lived for a considerable time at Pax Hill, Bentley, three miles from Farnham, with his wife, Olave, who founded the Girl Guides. Farnham has always had a number of Scout and Guide companies and here are Boy Scouts on a St George's Day parade, marching to St Thomas on the Bourne church, in the mid-1960s.

Unless children of today are introduced to history at an early age, it is potentially a subject which will be overlooked in the computer-dominated world of the twenty-first century. The children, aged six to twelve years, who attend the Museum of Farnham's Saturday club each month, often continue an interest in history, with several past members now specializing in the subject at university. Dressed in a genuine Victorian smock (often worn by working men for their wedding attire) and a 1932 wedding dress made from fabric swept up from a workroom floor, are a few club members in the 1990s.

In the spring of 1931, staff at St Andrew's School still educated infants and older girls up to the school-leaving age of fourteen years. A pupil in this group is Agnes Arras Keturah Tubb, who lived in St George's Road. She enjoyed acting and always took part in the school plays at Christmas. Soon after she left St Andrew's she was able to tread upon a larger stage when she took part in a fashion show at the Regal Cinema. Her unusual second name was due to having been born in 1917, during the First World War, when her father was fighting at Arras.

Nine
Fun and Games

Rosalind Trusler, aged six, skipping in the parish churchyard in 1970. Her father, Eddie, was a press photographer and came from a long-standing family of Truslers who lived in The Bourne. Today he lives in retirement on the Isle of Wight.

Wading in the Wey at Gostrey Meadow are a number of regulars from the Jolly Farmer (later the William Cobbett) public house, in fancy dress. The event was to commemorate Queen Elizabeth II's Coronation in 1953. The 'lady,' centre front, is holding a cask of Watney's Red Barrel. Older people might remember jokes about this brew, and with the rain, which was obviously falling at the time, plus the river in which the men are standing, they might consider this beer to be quite appropriate!

Children at the Bourne School, about forty years ago, enjoying themselves on adventure playground equipment paid for, and installed, through the hard work of the school's PTA.

Bourne Cub Scouts rode their 'hobby' horses at Farnham Castle for an event in connection with the Scouts' Diamond Jubilee in 1968. Their mothers made the horses and the costumes.

FARNHAM SCHOOL of CRICKET

ST. CROSS ESTATE,
EAST STREET, FARNHAM.

Professional : R. RELF *(Sussex).*

PROPRIETOR:

FRANK MOULDING.

SPORTS HOUSE. 29. BOROUGH. FARNHAM.

PHONE 975.

At one time Farnham had its own School of Cricket, which operated from St Cross Estate, just behind the present Seven Stars public house. Its proprietor was Frank Moulding, who also ran a sports shop at 29 The Borough, later to be taken over by Clark's Sports and Radio. This brochure advises the public that the club's professional is R. Self, who played for Sussex. Interestingly, for its period, the advertising material advises potential clients that 'a session will be arranged for ladies' – if required. The fee for a course of eight lessons was two guineas, payable in advance.

The open-air swimming pool in South Street, here seen in use, was paid for by public subscription to commemorate Queen Victoria's Diamond Jubilee. All that remains of the pool today are the arches, which were designed by Farnham architect Harold Falkner. The other reminder of the site's former use is a life-size sculpture of a small boy, shivering in swimming trunks and with a towel around his shoulders, which stands in Victoria Gardens behind the Falkner arches.

Happy faces at a Langham's Social Club and *Herald* Christmas party, in Church House, 29 January 1966, when an Oranges and Lemons arch was made by Lesley Morris, left, and Beverlie Martin. Harold Cole, who started with the company when he was fourteen, eventually became a director of the firm, but not before he had had his head 'chopped off' in the party game.

Pictures of the Coronation Day celebrations in Farnham in 1953, are few and far between, as many people found when trying to plan a Golden Jubilee display in 2002. Here the Farnham Coronation Queen (above), with her young page and two attendants, is watched by a large crowd who were kept well back from the dais. Far less formal, and probably more fun, is the large group of competitors at the Baldreys Coronation fancy dress party (below) – one little girl even turned up as New Zealand lamb.

Four, three and two-wheeled vehicles are lined up in this photograph, taken in Farnham about eighty years ago by Evelyn 'Jo' Simmonds, a daughter of Police Superintendent Simmonds of Farnham police station. The exact location is not known, apart from that it is in the Farnham area and that those featured are from this town.

Farnham Angling Society in the 1920s. Albert King, who established the society in 1912, is third from the right in front row and George Gunstone, who had started the Farnham District Anglers several years earlier, is also in the photograph, although his position is unidentified.

A sponsored swim was held in around 1970 to raise money for changing rooms at Bourne School and, amongst others, Ian and Richard Martin and Brian Castle took part. The event cost Esmé Martin dearly because she sponsored her boys at 6d a length. Richard gave up willingly after a few lengths but Martin, who had only just learned to swim, kept on going until his brother told him to stop because he was costing their mum too much money.

Outside the Bricklayer's Arms, Weydon Lane, the contestants who had taken part in the fancy-dress event organized for the Coronation party of Queen Elizabeth II, in 1953, line up for the cameraman.

Three times a year a fair was held in Castle Street, and local author George Sturt describes these days better than anyone else could do in his *A Small Boy in the Sixties*. This photograph was taken about seventy-five years later than George's memories of the fairs as places of merriment and laughter, with a steam-driven merry-go-round with galloping horses, and where ladies were, 'Specially invited' to roll coins down onto a marked board to try to win sixpence.

As Farnham Town's football team met only a stone's throw from West Street Council Boys' School it is feasible that some of the footballers featured on this postcard taken in the 1930/31 season had been pupils at that school. Farnham Town played on the ground beside the Memorial Hall. Some of this team seem to have had trouble with their knees, for at least three have protection – two on their left knees and one on his right.

Beaming smiles from Will Bowes and his father, as they proudly show the cannonballs which they found in Farnham Park. Taken around 1970, this happy pair were caught on camera by the late Edward Griffith who, in addition to being a press photographer, also ran a photographic studio in Downing Street.

Ten
Pen, Paint and Paper

This line-drawing of a derelict timber-framed building at Heath End was developed from a site colour sketch made by Randal Bingley in November 1965. As a youngster Randal lived close to this building and as well as being an artist he has written a book, *Where Dips The Sudden Jay*, about the Heath End area of his childhood. The building, of possible Tudor origin, faced south-south-east, in the grounds of a former Army college (now Hillcrest) and flanking Upper Weybourne Lane. When Randal sketched the cottage he said that it had undergone conversion to a domestic garage with wide double doors inserted at the rear. One early leaded casement remained and he believed the red brick infill was possibly a Georgian feature, contemporary with its modification from a good, minor homestead to a pair of cottages. Whether the garden well-head frame was a genuine utilitarian survival or a late ornamental fancy is unknown.

WINDSOR ALMSHOUSES, FARNHAM, AD. 1619

Here is an original watercolour by Bill Ewbank Smith, local government employee, author of three books about Farnham's history, which he gleaned from newspapers and council records, and an artist of some considerable standing in the local community. This is his impression of the seventeenth-century Andrew Windsor almshouses, in Castle Street, which he painted before the eight units were gutted internally and turned into the current four dwellings.

No. 200.   SEPTEMBER, 1905.

THE·FRENSHAM PARISH·MAGAZINE

S.ͭ MARY'S·CHURCH·FRENSHAM

Farnham:
Published by John Nichols, Borough.

Parish magazines are a wonderful storehouse of information for historians. This line drawing, on the cover of a *Frensham Parish Magazine* from more than a century ago, shows that the artwork, as well as the information, is worth noting.

Although Freemasonry is still a subject about which there is much secrecy, nevertheless the William Cobbett Lodge No. 7914, which meets in the Freemasons' Hall in Castle Street, is well known; the group has many members in the town. This logo appeared regularly, in the past, on dinner menus of Installation meetings.

87

In 1921 Farnham's greatest boxer, Neil 'Boy' McCormick, fought Ted 'Kid' Lewis, but unfortunately lost. The *Daily Mail* featured the match in a cartoon by its artist, Tom Watson. National newspapers took great interest in Farnham's boxer and when there was no 'hot' news their journalists sometimes invented it. Thus, on one occasion, a reporter published a tale about the people of Farnham being divided over whether or not 'Boy' McCormick should continue to be allowed to spar in Church House, a building dedicated to the Glory of God. The Rector of Farnham insisted that the reporter concerned came down from London to see him about the matter. He then sent the reporter back to town with nothing more than his statement that in the cleric's view a healthy man's body was equal, in the eyes of the Lord, to that of a beautiful flower.

Opposite: East Street once had two cinemas, The Regal and The County. The latter was demolished to make way for J. Sainsbury and the former was unceremoniously demolished, almost overnight and without permission, in 1986. In May 1992, a board which had been erected around the derelict site was decorated with this picture. Designed by architect Harold S. Scott and built of locally-made red bricks, the beautiful Art Deco building had been reduced to rubble by the method shown. In 2002 a cinema for East Street was under discussion. Older residents of the town laughed, ironically, at such a plan.

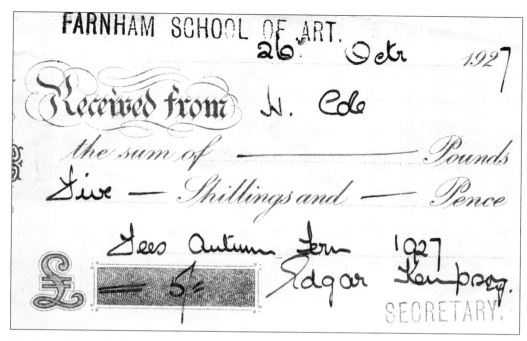

FARNHAM SCHOOL OF ART.

26. Octr 1927

Received from H. Cole

the sum of ———————— Pounds

Five — Shillings and — Pence

Fees autumn term 1927

Edgar Kempsey.

SECRETARY.

On the surface it did not cost a lot to take adult classes in art, but it must be remembered that when young Harold Cole paid his fee of five shillings at Farnham School of Art for the autumn term of 1927, he was earning less than 15 shillings per week at the *Farnham Herald*. He started art classes just eight days after his fourteenth birthday.

FARNHAM URBAN DISTRICT COUNCIL ELECTION

SATURDAY, 11th MAY, 1968

VOTE FOR

SCRAGG

AND

WILLIAMS

YOUR **LABOUR** CANDIDATES FOR
CASTLE WARD

TRANSPORT: IF YOU NEED TRANSPORT TO AND FROM THE POLLING BOOTH PLEASE RING
FARNHAM 3610

Published by Mr. R. E. Pocock, 33 Folly Hill, Farnham, and printed by Langhams Herald Press, West Street, Farnham.

John Scragg, 23, and Roy Williams, 46, stood as Labour candidates for the Castle Ward in the Farnham Urban District Council election of May 1968. Whilst Mr Scragg was a civil servant in the Ministry of Technology, Roy Williams, a father or four, was a Lieutenant-Commander in the RNVR and the RNR and had served in the Royal Navy during the Second World War. His wife Diana, a schoolteacher, also once stood for Labour, contesting a seat in the Bourne Ward.

One of the public houses most frequented by the town's vast art student population is The Plough, West Street. However, since the early 1990s it has also been known as The Scream, after the pub sign a student painted for it. Another student, Paul Cross, was given the opportunity to brighten up the interior with murals and this was the result. Paul also doubled as a local postman and did voluntary work at the Museum of Farnham.

When John Michael (Mike) Hawthorn brought the World Motor Racing Championship to Britain for the first time in 1958 the town rejoiced, and the Farnham Urban District Council members gave a dinner on 19 November in his honour. Held at the Bush Hotel, it included grapefruit cocktail, fried fillet of sole and roast Aylesbury duck. Entertainment, after the meal, was provided by Mary Joynes, founder of the Farnham Girls' Choir, accompanied by Maureen Beeken, whose father was a master at Farnham Grammar School. Unfortunately Mike Hawthorn died two months later when his car slewed off the road near Guildford and he hit a tree.

Dinner

given by the

FARNHAM URBAN DISTRICT COUNCIL

in honour of

Mr. John Michael Hawthorn

———

The Bush Hotel, Farnham

Wednesday, 19th November, 1958.

———

The Chairman of the Council
(Councillor C. W. Williams, J.P.)
in the Chair

In 1977 there were many Farnham street parties held to celebrate the Silver Jubilee of Queen Elizabeth II. One such event took place at 3 Waverley Lane, where the large garden was more than big enough to host the children from Broomleaf Road, including Rebecca Weeks, to whom this certificate was given.

THE PUBLIC HEALTH ACT, 1875.

FARNHAM.

WHEREAS the Urban District Council of Farnham have applied to the Local Government Board for sanction to borrow £100 for the widening and improvement of Station Hill, and sums amounting to £1.500 for the provision of a Recreation Ground between South Street and Long Bridge and for the purchase of land at Timberclose, near Factory Yard, for purposes of a Children's Playground:

AND WHEREAS the Local Government Board have directed Inquiry into the subject-matter of such Applications:

NOTICE IS HEREBY GIVEN that E. W. Hollingworth, Esquire, A.M.I.C.E., the Inspector appointed to hold the said Inquiry, will attend for that purpose at the Town Hall, Farnham, on Wednesday, the Twenty-eighth day of April, 1909, at Ten o'clock in the Forenoon, and will then and there be prepared to receive the evidence of any persons interested in the matter of the said Inquiry.

S. B. PROVIS,
Secretary.

Local Government Board,
14th April, 1909.

Printed by WATERLOW BROS. & LAYTON, LIMITED, 24 and 25, Birchin Lane, London, E C. (63863) Wt 53-80 80 4-09

Almost a century ago the idea was mooted, under the Public Health Act, that open spaces should be secured for the benefit of the town's residents. Gostrey Meadow was the result although, as this poster states, land at Timber Close, in The Hart, was also under consideration for the same purpose.

This wall painting, to be found in one of the upper rooms at Vernon House, West Street, was used for the cover illustration of the 1967 Farnham Festival Programme. The words which can be seen are part of the metrical version of Psalm 103. Above the script are the arms of Bishop Horne, Bishop of Winchester from 1561 to 1580. A scholar himself, he apparently had a licence from Queen Elizabeth I for a school to be erected in Farnham and it is believed that this could be Farnham Grammar School. The Farnham Festival was once an annual event in the town and enabled young people to perform specially commissioned pieces.

A Farnham bank note dated 1815, on which John Cock & Co. promise to pay the bearer one pound.

A CORNER OF THE COFFEE ROOM.

A CORNER OF THE DRAWING ROOM.

Taken from *Farnham Past and Present*, written in 1900 by Arthur Hart, these drawings show how little the Oak Lounge and restaurant at the Bush Hotel have changed in the past century. The Bush is Farnham's oldest hostelry and was one of old coaching inns where the Red Rover, Collyer's Coach and others would set down and pick up passengers. Many have written about the Bush, including William Makepeace Thackeray, in *The Virginians*. In the reign of James I (1603-25) a Mr Harding, who kept the Bush, had a warrant issued against him by Sir George Mompesson, demanding that Mr Harding show under what authority he operated without the King's licence. Other services available to patrons in 1900 have vanished today, including the tennis courts, the bowling greens and the free-of-charge lock-up for visitors' bicycles, but then, too, the terms have changed. For example, in 1900 a hip bath, in one's bedroom, cost an extra one shilling on the bill, the same price that was charged for afternoon tea.

Marshall Barnes, a local artist, pictured many scenes of the town but this is one of his lesser-known drawings and shows young children going into the pupils' entrance of St George's School, which once operated from the centre and left of this building. When the school moved into larger premises (first at Pierrepont and later at Frensham Heights), No. 70 Castle Street once more became a private house, whose owner, Maggie Fawkes, was a local councillor in the 1980s.

During 2002 planning permission was sought by developers to demolish the Black Prince public house, in Upper Hale Road, which had dispensed alcoholic beverages for over 150 years. It was to be replaced with houses. This drawing of the building was made by Jim McDonald Good, a former licensee at the Black Prince. He gave it to his customers as a Christmas card.

FARNHAM'S LAST CHANCE?

THE FLYOVER

A PUBLIC MEETING

Wednesday, August 6th, 1969
at 8.00 p.m.

At Church House, Union Road, Farnham

ALL WELCOME

MEETING SPONSORED BY THE FARNHAM SOCIETY

The success of this meeting is vital to getting a

PUBLIC INQUIRY

Published by S. H. Anderson. St. Christoph, Boundstone.
P. M. Gibbons, 3 Little Austins, Farnham.

Langham, Herald Press, Farnham 102/7/69

A public meeting was called to discuss proposals for road improvements at Hickley's Corner – and the town's residents were told that it was the last chance they would have to have their say about the notorious traffic junction. This was thirty-three years ago – but to date nothing has changed!

Farnham Urban District Council

CASTLE WARD

SATURDAY, MAY 11th, 1968

BE INDEPENDENT

and vote for

AN INDEPENDENT WOMAN CANDIDATE

V. G. KING

If you agree that Party Politics should not influence Local Government

VOTE INDEPENDENT

VOTE

KING	X

If you need a car to bring you to the poll, please let me know at 18 Beavers Road, Telephone Farnham 6390

Printed by Langham's, Herald Press, 114 West Street, Farnham, and Published by V. G. King, 18 Beavers Road, Farnham

Miss Vicky King was educated at Farnham Girls' Grammar School and later became a teacher, spending many years at Hale school. She served on many committees, including the WEA, the Save the Children fund and the Ramblers' Association, and was on the board of directors of the Castle Theatre. She was an independent woman, never shirking from making a stand on a subject of which she believed was important.

Eleven
Bits and Pieces

Until the River Wey was widened in Farnham in the mid-1960s, it regularly broke its banks, often flooding halfway up this street. Traffic was still two-way at that time. Priest's Typewriter Services, right, is now a fish and chip shop and Southern Rentals, next door, is currently the award-winning Sterling Sandwich Bar.

History dating back at least 8,000 years is encompassed in this aerial view of the Shepherd and Flock roundabout taken by Aerofilms on 27 June 1969. To the right of the top roundabout is the Middle Stone Age pit dwellings site, deemed to be the oldest village in this country so far discovered. Just out of view on the right are the remains of a Bronze Age burial ground. To the left of the large roundabout is Bourne Mill, mentioned in *Domesday Book*, and slightly above centre is the site of a Roman villa and bath. In the upper left area can be seen part of Farnham Park and just out of shot is The Avenue, which is believed to be the remains of an Iron Age road. The buildings, centre, have all been demolished to make way for houses and a health centre. The Farnham Workhouse is visible and a few prefabricated buildings, constructed immediately after the Second World War in Roman Way, still remain, although they were demolished soon after this picture was taken. The majority had, by this time, already been demolished and only their footings can be seen.

Moses Parratt was born on 5 July 1839. On 11 May 1862 he married Elizabeth Coleman in Odiham. The couple lived at Boundstone and had five children, Annie, Esau, Elizabeth, Kate and Moses. This photograph of Moses senior shows him in his working clothes – but possibly his best boots, as they are well polished – and he has a pair of studded working boots slung over his shoulder with the tools of his trade. In his right hand is the all-important liquid refreshment in a stoneware jar, of vital necessity when carrying out a hard day's work loading hay, which is suggested by the pitchfork.

Most villages had a postcard produced during the First World War showing Rolls of Honour – the names of every person (mostly men) who had left their homes to fight for their country. Tilford was no exception. In 1919 a war memorial was erected in the church giving the names of twenty-seven of the men who were killed. After the Second World War a tablet was added naming twenty-three parishioners who died on active service between 1939-45.

When Maurice Macmillan died in 1984, Virginia Bottomley became the Conservative MP for South West Surrey and for the first time Farnham residents found themselves with a female Member of Parliament – one of only twenty-five women in the Commons at that time. With her husband Peter, also an MP, and their family, she moved to Milford. Virginia was frequently seen in Farnham and occasionally Peter joined her – on this occasion they are in Elphick's. Virginia is speaking to Allan Elphick whilst Peter is left holding her flowers!

When a bust to William Cobbett (radical politician, author and originator of *Hansard*, the daily record of happenings in Parliament) was first erected, it was placed in Gostrey Meadow, left, only a few yards from his birthplace, the Jolly Farmer inn, now known as the William Cobbett. However, the bust was soon vandalized and, upon its restoration, the commemorative object was relocated to the garden of the Museum of Farnham.

The people standing in the porch are probably thinking that it was bad enough to have to go to the doctor (the building has been a doctor's surgery for over 100 years) without being marooned there. On the left are the Vacuum Cleaner Shop and The Corner Cake Shop, the latter owned and run by a Miss Winter.

One tiny semi-circular window on the premises of Michael Sargeant, photographer, in the background, is all that really gives a clue as to the exact location of this 1980s photograph. Tim Phillips was engaged to march around town wearing billboards promoting a new market which for a short while ran weekly in the old Watney, Combe and Reid yard, now part of the St Georges Courtyard development. The entrance to the yard is adjacent to the present Pizza Express and the brewery name can still be discerned on the wooden bar which stretches from this Italian restaurant to the off-licence on the other side.

Looking westwards along Bridgefield in the winter of 1962/63. In Farnham the snow started to fall on Boxing Day 1962 and the last patches vanished from Hungry Hill and Rowhills Copse, at Heath End, in April 1963. Former Farnham resident Robin Broatch, now living in Australia, sent this photograph back to Farnham especially for this volume.

When Kay Crowe moved to Farnham in 1965, the town did not have a single charity shop. She opened the first Oxfam unit in East Street in 1967, later moving to the South Street shop featured here. This was later demolished to make way for Les Smith's. After two further moves the charity moved into The Woolmead, where it remains. Kay, mother of four, was a tireless worker for causes in which she and her husband Tony believed, and was delighted, in October 1969, when it was published that the Farnham branch of Oxfam made £2,400 profit in the previous year – an impressive sum in those days.

A shivering cherub on an ice-covered pool in the Bush Hotel garden is a complete contrast to a sundial on the ceiling of the hotel's lounge. However, there is a connection. The time could once be told by using the sundial inside the building, when the original pool was located outside the lounge's window. For safety it was moved to its present position, which gives a more picturesque winter scene.

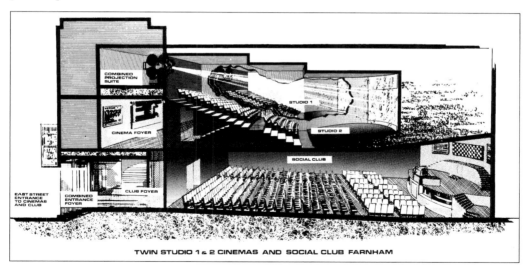

TWIN STUDIO 1 & 2 CINEMAS AND SOCIAL CLUB FARNHAM

When films failed to fill the Regal's cinema seats, it underwent several changes of ownership, style and name. This artist's impression of the Farnham Entertainment Centre divided the first floor into two cinema studios and left the stalls below for the Star Bingo and Social Club. The building was unceremoniously closed in September 1985, and demolished a few months later. Ironically, in 2002, part of the East Street regeneration plan includes the possibility of a new cinema on virtually the same site.

Willmer House, West Street, since 1960 the home of the Museum of Farnham, is a Grade I listed Georgian building. Since it was built in 1718 it has been home to a hop-grower, a dentist, a canon, a boarding school for girls and a school for boys as well as being a billet for Canadian soldiers in the Second World War. This photograph, taken when it was a private house, shows the housekeeper standing in the doorway of the annexe (now the museum's library) which was her home.

Until the 1960s, when its banks were widened, the River Wey frequently flooded its banks. This peaceful scene, photographed a century ago, shows the water touching the walls of part of the former Bridge Inn, adjacent to the river on the eastern side of Longbridge.

This church, now known as the United Reformed church, in South Street, was dedicated in 1872. In 1893 the large hall and vestry were added and in 1929 the vestry was replaced by the present ancillary rooms. In 1981 the Victoria Road entrance was built and at the same time a small layby was constructed on this side of the church. In 1792 the Congregationalists in Farnham opened the Ebenezer Chapel in East Street (now part of Swain and Jones' car display area), but a century later their numbers had outgrown this building and, at a cost of £4,836, the church featured here was constructed by Goddard and Sons, Farnham builders of East Street. However, it took until 1908 before the final debt on building the church was cleared when £405 was raised at Ye Olde English Fayre held in the Town Hall and Corn Exchange buildings.

During the First World War a sign over an arch of the old Town Hall and Corn Exchange building at the foot of Castle Street informs everyone that part of the building was used as a 'Soldiers Recreation, Writing and Refreshment Room'. Just inside the archway in the centre of the picture, was the town's water conduit. Today a small part of an iron ring in a paving stone is all that remains of this once-important asset.

Mr Shrubb, a Farnham photographer who had a studio in The Borough and a shop in East Street, is believed to have taken this picture of the May Queen and Maypole dancers at The Bourne just before the start of the First World War. The children are all dressed in their best white dresses and probably tried very hard with the difficult twists of the maypole ribbons. However, from the number of adult heads which are looking elsewhere than at the children, it would seem that little interest was being shown in their efforts.

Only the small tree on the right gives any hint of where this photograph was taken in the early 1980s. Expedier House, formerly in Union Road, adjacent to Gostrey Meadow, was demolished at great expense, to be replaced by the present office complex. This stood empty for several years after its construction, although the launch day provided by the marketing agents included a lavish reception complete with a string quartet of young ladies in evening dresses.

F. Sturt, bookseller, stationer and newsagent traded from 42 The Borough for many years. In addition to the items already mentioned this shop also stocked Arcadian Heraldic Ware, similar to the famous Goss china pieces. In Farnham, however, these were exclusive to Lintern and Peters, almost opposite Sturt's, so the bookseller – who also published his own postcards – had to make do with the less prestigious chinaware.

This photographic postcard was posted on 7 June 1951 and the sender was about to go to London to see the attractions at the Festival of Britain. The plane tree, centre, was one of those planted to commemorate Queen Victoria's Diamond Jubilee, in 1897. The sign which can just be seen on a lamp standard behind the tree, points to the public conveniences which were once in Park Row. Near to a group of schoolboys and their master is a street-cleaner's cart but no cleaner. Perhaps he had called into the Nelson Arms for a 'swift half'.

Special events have long been commemorated with the planting of a tree and it was a case of decorated shovels to the fore at this ceremony, in Tilford, to mark the Coronation of Queen Elizabeth II on 2 June 1953.

The 1960s saw a number of do-it-yourself projects carried out by parents of schoolchildren and parishioners of various schools and churches. Here, digging the foundations of St Martin's Hall, The Bourne, is a group of volunteers including Mrs Baker, Pat Baker, Barbara Daniels and Mr Moorcroft.

Photography was in its infancy when this now very rare photograph of the tower of Farnham parish church was taken in 1865. Within weeks building work began, to raise the tower to its present height. It was not until 1839 that the word photography was used for what was then a new art. One wonders who was the elderly woman, seen in the right foreground, or what she would have felt had she ever seen her likeness captured by the new-fangled method.

Looking like the little boxes on the hillside made famous in a song thirty-five years ago, here are the houses at Sandy Hill, Hale, before time and vegetation had mellowed them. On the extreme left are the trees surrounding St Mark's cemetery. The 'Monopoly-type' houses leading from the right to centre, are on Alma Way.

The large stage and magnificent curtains of the Regal Cinema provided a near-perfect backdrop for fashion shows, put on by local dress shops, for the benefit of Farnham ladies. Miss Agnes Tubb, aged seventeen, worked at such a shop and appeared as a bride in this finale of the show held in 1934, an event held soon after the cinema was built. In those days there was a superstition that if you posed as a bride when you were single you would never marry. Fortunately Miss Agnes broke with superstition and later married Mr R. Trust.

Young Agnes Arras Keturah Tubb earned a number of articles in local newspapers about her performances in school concerts. In a 1929 *Farnham Herald* report about her role in *The Woodland Princess*, she is described as being: 'Perhaps the most outstanding figure in the cast [as] The Fairy. This girl has not only the natural prettiness one associates with the fairy but she possesses a fine, clear voice and her elocution is above the average for a girl of her age... Her assurance – which was of a natural and pleasing kind – never failed her'.

Farnham West Street Council Boys' School is just one of eight names that the school on this site has held since it first opened in 1896. The others are: West Street Board School, West Street Boys' School, The Castle County Junior Boys' School, St Andrew's Junior Mixed School, St Andrew's Church of England Middle School, Potter's Gate Church of England (Controlled) First and Middle School and currently Potter's Gate CE Primary School. The boys excelled not only at swimming but at other sports as well, in 1927, hence the three different types of clothing worn by them. At the time this photograph was taken Mr H.T. Meddows Taylor was the head. He held this position there from 1914-31.

Standing together at the official opening of the Borelli Yard development in 1988 are old and new mayors. On the left is Gordon James, at his last function as Farnham town mayor and on the right stands Alan Lazarus, the mayor of Waverley, at one of his first events after taking office.

Farnham United Breweries had its own football team, known as The Bungs, who played on the ground, in West Street, adjacent to the brewery and now part of the Crosby Way complex. Here the team of 1910 is posing outside what was known as the Lion Brewery.

Farnham's Council Chamber is a magnificent room, yet few people see it unless they attend a public council meeting. The building in which the chamber is housed was opened by the Archbishop of Canterbury in 1903. Standing is Town Mayor, Councillor Harry Lawrence, on his right is the town clerk, Fred Culver, and on his left Gordon James, who was also later to become a Farnham town mayor.

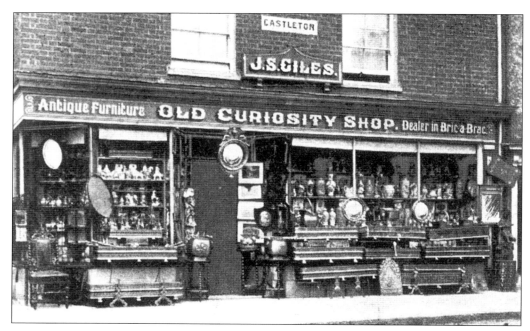

J.S. Giles owned shops in both Castle Street and South Street, and advertised them both in *Mates' Guide* during the early part of the twentieth century. The Castle Street premises (above) are now a dentist's surgery, while the South Street shop (below) was demolished to make way for Les Smith's motor accessories business. Later the right-hand side of this building was owned by Miss Tigwell, whose toyshop was a Mecca for most of the local children who had pocket money to spend. Today teeth, rather than curios, occupy the time of the present owner of the Castle Street building; he is a dentist.

Twelve
Down Your Way

Beneath the road in the foreground lie the foundations of a hostelry known as The Round House and although it does not look much like an inn, The Alliance (right, and now an estate agent's) replaced a much older pub by the same name. This scene, probably dating from the 1930s, shows Downing Street with two-way traffic and J.E. Spencer, who sold underclothing and was also a draper, silk mercer and costumier, occupying the premises on the left. Mr John Elliot Spencer (son of the firm's founder who first traded from this site in 1868), died in February 1949. He had attended Farnham Grammar School and been a founder member of the Rotary Club in Farnham from its formation in 1923.

Members of the Tily family occupied this site at 6 and 7 Castle Street from at least 1826 when John Tily, a patten and brushmaker, is listed as living there. By 1855 John and Mary Tily were running the premises as ironmongers. Mary and John also owned 117 West Street, which had earlier been Hart's ironmongery, but they withdrew from this in 1933. Tily's was also noted as a cycle dealer although it is not known whether the line-up in this photograph was to promote bicycles or just those used by customers or delivery lads. The name of Tily only disappeared from Castle Street towards the end of the twentieth century.

Established in 1760, W.W. Williams, wine merchant, at 122 West Street, advertised at the beginning of the twentieth century that it had 'competent cellar men available at all times to attend at Gentlemen's Private Cellars for all requisite purposes'. This shop faces the top of Downing Street and became the Junior Hammick's Bookshop in the 1980s before it was sold to a fashion firm.

For many years the name of Davies, in Farnham, was synonymous with newspapers and stationery. First there was a business at 121 East Street (now beneath The Woolmead complex, then at 11 Castle Street (now a dentist's surgery). This postcard was published by Davies Brothers, from the East Street address, and although the photograph was taken about ninety years ago, this view of West Street has changed only slightly with the post office, second from the left, having been rebuilt and the groceries from Kingham's (extreme right) being replaced by the sales of mobile phones.

A look along The Borough, west to east, December 1962. The shops with their Christmas tree lights look so much brighter than they do in the twenty-first century. Nearest the camera, on the right, is Hales the electricians, then Hamilton Jones, gents' outfitters, with the distinctive hat as its shop sign. Left is the sign for Alan Clarke, gents' hairdresser (which was under the Town Hall Buildings' arcade) and the newspaper vendor sign for W.H. Smith and Son Ltd. Traffic was still two-way in The Borough at that time.

The old Regal Cinema is marked in this aerial view of East Street. The northern part of the street was demolished over thirty years ago, so almost half the buildings in the photograph were pulled down, and as well as a new road being constructed where the broken line has been drawn, a row of concrete 'monstrosities' (as most people refer to the units) known as The Woolmead, was built. In October 2002 the site in the lower half of the picture was under the spotlight, and has been the subject of much investigation and discussion. In all probability, within two years the only buildings in this photograph to remain will be the double-ridged unit in the upper left corner and the flats for the elderly in the centre at the top.

A century ago the Conservative Club, in Ivy Lane, off Downing Street, was a corset factory. Despite this use, which, in Victorian times, was essentially dedicated to women, members of the fairer sex were unable to become members of the Farnham Conservative Club in their own right until the latter part of the twentieth century after Margaret Thatcher – who visited Farnham in 1985 and started the presses rolling for the printing of the *Surrey and Hants News* – had become Britain's first woman prime minister.

The type of perambulator, if nothing else, dates this photograph of the Co-operative Society's East Street shop to the late 1940s. Food is still served from this building but in the form of Chinese meals. Henri Liu has owned and run the Kar Ling Kwong restaurant here since 1964.

When Thomas Hill first moved into 19 Downing Street in 1912, he soon gained a position of prestige in the town because of the expert way in which he wired the homes of the richer residents for electricity and installed generators where necessary. His estimates were free (Farnham people have always appreciated something for nothing) and as well as working in lighting and heating, Mr Hill dealt in telephones, bells and electric light bulbs. Seventy years later, when the firm eventually closed down, it still occupied the same site, the same ceramic tiles and screen bordered the front window and the same heads were on the pillars at both sides of it. Only the front door and the style of lettering on the fascia board had changed. Even the down-pipe on the right of the older picture was still in exactly the same position in the 1980s.

Both W.H. Smith & Son Ltd and Boots (above) had Lending Libraries which helped to bring reading matter to the masses – and as a small fee was necessary in these establishments they were considered to be 'better' than public libraries. Later Boots took over a building a few doors farther west, hitherto owned by Timothy White's. The building pictured here is reputed to be haunted.

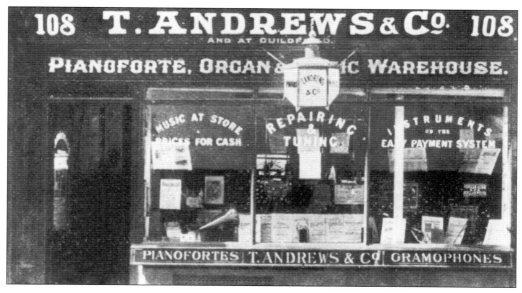

Sandwiched between Pullinger's and the Farnham post office in West Street was, for many years, T. Andrews and Co. music and record shop. This is a very old building and folklore has it that at the rear of the building was a room with a false ceiling, which was used by men signalling to others at the keep of Farnham Castle during the Civil War. It is certain that a grille existed twenty years ago, just beneath the roofline, which was in direct line to the castle, so there is really no reason to disbelieve this word-of-mouth story from the seventeenth century.

This photograph was taken about forty years ago, and there are few clues as to the whereabouts of the scene, apart from the small building at the back, right, the piece of brickwork, front left, and the River Wey flowing beneath the bridge. In the far distance, on the right, is the former Portsea Island Mutual Co-operative (PIMCO) furniture store. John Mills & Sons builders' merchants was demolished to make way for the present police station.

Once an area where carts and horses were protected for the night and later a thoroughfare for vehicles, as above, today the Lion and Lamb Yard is a pedestrian precinct. The yard is said to be one of the most haunted areas of Farnham. One of the double gates at the entrance to West Street has a smaller, single, gate set into it used, in the past, to enable pedestrians to enter the yard at night without the necessity of calling the nightwatchman to open the double gates.

Few would have thought that less than twenty years after its grand opening the Redgrave Theatre would be boarded up, vandalized and under threat of demolition. A superb walnut tree is on the extreme left and the white building to the rear is part of Brightwell House, formerly Lowlands, believed to be building where Florence Nightingale stayed the night before she left for the Crimean War.

One of the first Indian restaurants to open in Farnham, The Viceroy, situated almost opposite the Seven Stars, in East Street, served its first customers in November 1981. The building it took over had earlier been used by the local council as a rent office. The opening was organized at such speed that one of the local newspaper reporters there to cover the event helped out by hanging up the curtains. Mr Nur Monie stated, proudly, that his was the only Indian restaurant in south-east England to be in the 1983 *Good Food Guide*.

Today 1a The Borough is recognized as being the number on a door up to the side of No.1 – Clinton Cards. However, in the 1920s it would seem that Fredrick Privett operated from 1a, which had the West Street shop front. An advertisement from the early years of the twentieth century showed that Mr Privett was a 'shirt tailor, hosier, glover, hatter and an Indian and Colonial outfitter'. He also sold fancy waistcoats, travelling bags and rugs, hand and brief bags, hat cases, raincoats, mackintoshes and rainoffs! However, Mr Privett did not extend credit to his customers nor would he accept cheques. He states clearly in his advertisement, 'Terms strictly cash'.

S. Bates, situated at 29 The Borough, opposite the present W.H. Smith, was both a greengrocer and florist a century ago when this advertisement appeared in a *Mates' Guide* to Farnham.

Jim Bodkin, who still lives in Farnham, is proud of this photograph of his grandfather standing outside his Castle Street tailor's business. Grandad Bodkin arrived in Farnham from Canterbury in 1889 and bought the shop for £600. Jim was born above the retail outlet in a room which had once been the chapel of the building when it was run by nuns for pregnant, unmarried girls from London.

For 131 years there has been a shoe shop at 45 The Borough, and for most of that time it was known as Holden's. Interestingly, K shoes were sold in the shop in the first decade of the twentieth century, just as they continue to be in the first decade of the twenty-first.

Patrick's Stonemasons still have a funeral directors business in East Street, but at one time also ran a stonemason's firm from this showroom and workshop on the Guildford Road, adjacent to the present household waste site. Not only did this company make and engrave tombstones, they also had a brisk trade in marble fireplaces in the 1970s.

Very few people in Farnham like the architecture of the 1960s Woolmead complex, of which Mr Crusty was a part. However, without exception, everyone loved the bread and cakes made by Tom Cornwall, the genial, genuine baker who once operated from here. Unfortunately, high overheads eventually forced Mr Cornwall to take Mr Crusty's dough to a town ten miles from Farnham.

In the late 1970s and early eighties, Carole Anne Gilks ran a boutique in the 1930s parade of shops known as Bush House in South Street. Her name fitted well in the glass panels above the door, as can be seen in this picture, where she is standing in the entrance. Before Carole moved in, the shop was known as Four Seasons and owned by Bill Westerman. Carole's successor was David Roberts, as the Flying Printer, who remained in the building until early in 2002. In 1985 Carole married local author Guy Bellamy. They have one daughter, Kate.

Here is Fatties, which once operated from Downing Street. Some said that a name such as this, in the weight-conscious eighties, would be doomed to failure as a café, and it is true to say that it did not remain in business for long. 28b was subsequently home to another café, 'Grandma Buggins', and it might have been ageism which caused 'her' demise. Sultan's, the present owners of the food outlet here have been more successful and have traded for a number of years, but perhaps it is the fact that they remain open after the pubs have closed which has helped its longer survival.

Pine trees grew in abundance around the villages of Rowledge and Wrecclesham and, in the former village, Alice Holt Forest abuts the school and the church. This picture is believed to have been taken on land that was part of one of the large houses in Rowledge, and shows one worker with a watering can, another with a trug in which to put eggs he collects, one presumes. The gentlemen on the extreme right and left are probably their employers, one of whom is holding a chicken, which was perhaps destined to be on the dinner table that night.

Hart's Yard, leading off West Street, is, without doubt, the most colourful thoroughfare in the town throughout the entire year. Mrs Kay Pace is responsible for dozens of pots and troughs of bulbs, summer plants and autumn and winter greenery, all of which she waters and tends daily. Quiet and unassuming, Mrs Pace, pictured left, deserves public recognition for the part she has played, for at least the last twenty-five years, in keeping Farnham in bloom at all times.